the **TINY** book of

BIG
MANIFESTING

JEFFREY SEGAL

FOREWORD BY **DON JOSE RUIZ**

T0002373

Cover and interior design by Sky Peck Design
Cover art © iStock.com
Typeset in Mr Eaves San OT

Hampton Roads Publishing Company, Inc.
Charlottesville, VA 22906
Distributed by Red Wheel/Weiser, LLC
www.redwheelweiser.com

Sign up for our newsletter and special offers by going to
www.redwheelweiser.com.

ISBN: 978-1-64297-039-5
Library of Congress Cataloging-in-Publication Data available upon request.

Printed in the United States of America
IBI

10 9 8 7 6 5 4 3 2 1

To all my spiritual teachers and my mom,
my eternal gratitude for everything
you have blessed me with
and bestowed upon me.

Contents

Foreword

We all have a purpose here in this world.

We all have a purpose in this life, and when we are aware that we are life, and that we are a creating force, we begin to witness. We're here to manifest whatever is in our heart. Whatever we perceive, we begin to give it shape, to give it form, and to give it a story. That story is how we become the narrator of our life. When we find our voice to express what we have inside, there is no longer any doubt we can create what is in our inspired heart, then we will no longer sacrifice like we used to. When we wake up knowing that to create is the only thing that we need to be aware of in life, the only thing we have to do on our paths is to get out of our own way.

I remember feeling like I was in a labyrinth of creativity. Because I had suppressed myself, because I believed the lie that I wasn't a great artist, that I couldn't manifest whatever was within me because I wasn't good enough; I was less than. I turned my judgment, my excuses, my justification, my suppression into a belief system and gave that belief system life. I gave my power away—became haunted by guilt and shame, because I wasn't walking my path, because I was letting myself down. When I noticed I was getting in my own way, I realized I was robbing myself of the gift of creating what was in my heart. And when I figured that out, the Master told me: "You're also robbing this world of your full potential, your creativity. . . . When you believe in yourself, you can accomplish many things. But if you sabotage yourself, you can sabotage many things."

Imagine a painter that finishes a painting and looks at it and says it's not good. He says: "I'm an inadequate manifester," because he's always judging himself. Of course, he won't think anything he does is good because he doesn't have the awareness that everything is perfect. When we are aware that we're perfect just the way we are, we understand that the Divine Mother

Nature, God, whatever you believe it is that gave us this life, is the Master of Perfection. And the Master of Perfection makes us able to see into ourselves, knowing that we can have everything that we want in this world.

I'm so happy that my brother from spirit, Jeffrey Segal, has created *The Tiny Book of Book of Big Manifesting*, because it's in the art of creation where we see ourselves, because in the art of creation is our life. And on that path, we experience many life lessons. Brother Jeffrey Segal walks us along this path, so we can find ourselves in our own labyrinth, and not be corrupted or settle anymore, for a creation that wasn't right for us.

This is why, sometimes, our inspiration gets lost, because we don't believe that we can manifest anything in our life. And the most beautiful thing to manifest in our life is the freedom to create what's in our hearts. When we do this, we allow the love of our life to come out, just like it was a garden of roses finally coming into bloom. We're no longer suppressing them, instead we nurture them with water and sunshine. And, when we put our ideas out into the world, they're all perfect. But the moment we begin judging, our ideas, our manifestations, due to our own mental blocks, that is when we go against the infinite, because in the infinite is where dreams are born.

When we begin believing in ourself, we find the key. And this is what brother Jeffrey is sharing with us: how to find the art of creativity within us all, and to respect life as it is because life has its own rules, it has its own way of dreaming. When we, as in the Toltec tradition, don't take life personally, it has the freedom to create whatever it wants to create, because it has the freedom to create from a different world. And everyone has a world. The way I understand my world and belief system, I can activate the power to manifest. I can tell you one thing, we know that this planet is a small world, and that every individual is a creator, and that is what Toltec means, Artist of the Spirit, because we're creating art all the time; it's not a religion, it's a way of life, because we all work for the same boss.

I'm so happy for my brother, Jeffrey Segal, for writing this *Tiny Book of Big Manifesting*. To wake up all of the artists with the words of love that he expresses, and those words that are love will become like seeds. And to all you artists who are reading this, or listening to this, find your way and get inspired by this beautiful message of love.

Because this is our birthright, to be happy, to enjoy this life, to be authentic in ourself in good times and bad. And when the bad times come, we need to share our manifestations of love. When we share them with ourselves, we begin sharing them with others. This gives us the compassion to understand that life and death are the inspiration within the space between them. This is where we are—at the point in our lives where we can finally listen to ourselves without getting in the way, and realize that why we couldn't manifest is because we've been using words in a negative way to sabotage ourselves.

Imagine you had one day to manifest whatever is in your heart, to give yourself the most beautiful day. And then you go for it. You give yourself the permission to create and to listen to your inner self, your big, beautiful heart that is devoted to love. Now, with unconditional love in your whole being activated, you know that you're here on a mission, and that mission is to create whatever is within you and not get in the way anymore. Whatever your experiences in life, they will become the colors that you will paint onto the canvas of whatever project you choose. When you take action on what's in your imagination, you're not blocking it anymore because your spirit speaks to you. This is the beautiful thing about art. When artists heed inspiration from the infinite that is within, they begin truly listening without any self-importance, from an impersonal point of view.

You get inspired by your feelings, by your emotions, by manifesting your love, by overcoming any difficult times, and by getting inspired by those difficult times to create your art.

You can say to yourself that this is just a dream. And if you don't like your dream, you can change it. How? Because it's your dream. That's the power of believing in yourself. Because if you don't believe in yourself, how can you manifest?

. . .

When you believe in yourself, you can manifest. But not because you believe you are more powerful than anybody else. No. That's ego. The real power is when you listen to you, and have all the faith you need to create whatever is inside of you and to dismiss any lies that will sabotage you. In that moment, you begin noticing that you are now in a position to create whatever is in your heart because you can manifest.

With brother Jeffrey Segal's guide, he will take you through a journey through the art of creation and his "Code of Life." Because when you balance these two, you have respect for all creation, including yourself. Remember, you are love, and you are meant to be loved by yourself, because you're grateful to be alive. And when you're grateful to be alive, you know that the body you have belongs to this planet Earth, the divine mother of life itself. We are the energy that holds the space to create. This is why we're here in life—to experience, to see all the beauty and all the hard times, and turn hell into heaven, suffering into happiness, as we bring our light to them. That is the gift of manifesting. Because when we live this way, we bring light and heaven into creative freedom, to walk in the labyrinth of creation that is this world, freely, without believing in lies and sacrificing the loves of our lives anymore. So, it's time to wake up, brothers and sisters. And I'm not sorry to say, once you wake up, you can never go back to sleep. Now I invite you to go on a journey, a journey of infinite potential, surrender, and letting go, and to the beginning of manifesting the art of your life.

Amen.

—don Jose Ruiz,
author of *The Medicine Bag* and
The Wisdom of the Shamans

Introduction

You're looking for a book. You're looking for some wisdom, some advice, something to inspire you, to move you along your path, to take you to the next level. You've picked up this book and are thinking: "Why should I read this one?" or "Can this book help me? Does this book have what I'm looking for?"

I have about thirty seconds to answer these questions and convince you to buy this book and read on.

If you are looking to change your life, to add to your life, to bring relationships and experiences into your life that have been missing, then the answer to these questions are: "Yes, this book can help you. I have used the principles that will follow to create the life I have always wanted—both personally and professionally." No joke. No BS.

There have been ups and downs. There have been challenges: in relationships, in career, and in health. But the key is that these challenges have been manageable, short-lived, and in the end, for my better good, and for my growth. This is what challenges, struggles, hardships, whatever you want to call them, are for: to aid in one's growth so that you get more of what you want.

That is the purpose of this book. To help you get more of what you want, what you desire, what you dream of. If that's what you're looking for, then this is the book for you.

Hopefully, I've got you now. If you want to read on, or just need a bit more convincing, here's a bit more about me.

I'm in my early sixties. I currently own the largest spiritual bookstore in Los Angeles, Mystic Journey Bookstore. Although the bookstore opened in October 2008, right at the beginning of The Great Recession, it is now a thriving success. I opened the Mystic Journey after being a highly successful, multimillion dollar generating lawyer for over twenty-five years. But

I didn't just decide one day to ditch the law practice and open a bookstore.

Rather, after wanting to leave the practice of law for over a decade, the Universe decided, with my help of course, to let me experience a bout with cancer to help me make the decision. The encounter with cancer led me to one of the most important decisions of my life—to follow my intuition and not undergo recommended chemotherapy after the doctors discovered a post-operative abnormality in my lymph nodes, and instead pursue an alternative, natural course of healing. The abnormality disappeared, and I have been cancer free for over a decade.

Then, a few years ago, I became the founder of the largest crystal gallery in all of Southern California, if not the United States or even the world; a showroom of magnificent crystals and geodes, some standing over seven feet tall or weighing more than two-thousand pounds. This business came about solely from my mental powers of creation.

After opening Mystic Journey Bookstore, I thought about opening a second bookstore for many years. A few opportunities came my way, but nothing materialized. At the same time, my interest in crystals grew and I began bringing larger crystals into the bookstore. Soon, however, I was running out of space for large crystals and I began to think, "I wish I had more space." As my interest in large crystals grew, however, my interest in opening a second bookstore waned. I became stuck with an ever-growing desire for bigger crystals. My deep desire was to have a crystal gallery, a large, open retail space, like an art gallery, right next to the bookstore. But this could not happen where the bookstore was located as on one side was a residential property, and on the other was a restaurant space. Eventually, I threw my hands up, and more or less gave up trying to figure out a solution.

Then, out of the blue, I got a call from the bookstore's landlord. He said, "I have this new space that has become available. You have told me about wanting to have more big crystals. I think this place would be perfect." It was not next to the bookstore, or even on the same street, but it was nearby, about a mile away. While it was not exactly what I had desired or envisioned, I took the leap, the step forward, and a month later Mystic Journey Crystal Gallery was born.

But as so often happens, this was not the end of the story. My lease for the bookstore was set to end in the spring of 2020. Due to crazily rising rents on the street where my bookstore was founded, Abbot Kinney Blvd. in Venice, California, I decided in 2019 that I had to move to a new location. I was sad about this, as the bookstore had been on Abbot Kinney for twelve years and had been very successful. But this was something I felt I had to do to ensure the continued success, and even survival, of the Mystic Journey Bookstore. Surprisingly, (but really not surprisingly), on the first day I went to look for a new retail location with my commercial real estate broker, I found what I thought was the perfect space. It was on a wonderful retail street, Main Street in Santa Monica, California, that was the ideal size, with an amazing garden patio and at the right rental price. I signed a new lease within days, right at the beginning of 2020, and figured I was set for our move in late spring of 2020. But then the Covid-19 pandemic hit.

I shut the bookstore down a month sooner than planned. But this shutdown gave us time to do our build-out in the new location and make our move. Amazingly, (but not amazingly), during this time of shutdown, which also included the shutdown of the crystal gallery, I was approached by the owner of the business next to our new bookstore location, inquiring whether I would be interested in sub-letting their location as they could not survive the pandemic closure. And there it was, manifesting right before my eyes. The opportunity to have the crystal gallery right next door to my bookstore. It took a little longer than expected, but I had and held this vision, and I made it happen. I made it manifest. And the new Mystic Journey Bookstore and Mystic Journey Crystal Gallery are now one, side by side, next to each other. (I also have to add, the business which was in the space that the crystal gallery now occupies was called Bryn Walker, and my daughter's name is Brin—not the most common name. What is the chance of that? Divine intervention?)

And now, I've had two very successful careers, and I'm working (if you can call it that), at the job of *my* choice; at the career I, me, myself chose out of any possible second career.

In relationships, I consider myself to have been very successful as well. When I married nearly thirty years ago, I used the principles in this book to bring in the perfect wife at the time; she was exactly what I wanted. We had a wonderful marriage for many years, had a beautiful home, created a beautiful daughter, and traveled the world. But nothing stays the same, and the relationship changed, and after some twelve years of marriage, I, like so many, went through a divorce. It was not easy, but as far as divorces go, it was quite manageable, if not amicable.

When one goes through a divorce and comes out the other side, the question is often asked: "What happened? What would I want different in my next partner that was lacking in my just-ended relationship?" I answered this question and asked the Universe for a new partner with the specific qualities I desired. This request was answered, and the Universe brought the perfect partner to aid me though my cancer and help me open Mystic Journey.

Years later, this relationship also ended. Again I asked the Universe for someone with specific qualities, qualities that I felt were needed in the next phase of my life. The Universe delivered again, providing me with just the relationship I wanted, and I'm still in that relationship more than ten years later.

I'm not making this up. I asked for a partner, a woman with certain, specific qualities for a long term relationship three times now. Each time, I've received just what I asked for. And while two of these relationships have ended, they were perfect, just what I needed at the time, just like my current relationship. You can have the relationship you want, too.

Finally, beyond my professional life and the personal relationships I've had in my life, I also have what I would call my "external," or environmental life. And in this aspect of my life, I have exactly, and I mean *exactly* what I want as well. I live in my dream home; a condo on the beach. I travel the world; I've visited some fifty countries. And I have a fabulous, independent, self-supportive, twenty-something daughter with whom I have a great, but not overbearing relationship.

I share all this not to gloat, but to do my best to say to you: I wrote this book to share with you the principles I've learned, and the philosophies and values that I hold and that I've used to create everything I've ever wanted in my life. And I believe that if you use what I share in this book, you can create all you want in your life as well. I've lived it. I'm a living example of how you can create whatever you want in your life. I'm not perfect. No one is. But I've had, and continue to have, a great bleeping life. And you can, too.

Two last notes. First, while I will be sharing practical steps and actual practices that you can use in your life to create all that you want, there is another part of the work that will facilitate, enhance, and accelerate your creative abilities. In fact, without also implementing this second part of the work, the creative process can be at best, stymied, and at worst, brought to a complete standstill. This second part of the work is what I call a "Code of Life." It is a set of values, a set of principles to live by, as you move through each day and each moment. Both the practices and the principles are needed to manifest your truest desires and live the life you dreamed of. You can undertake all the "manifesting practices" you want, try out every approach to or ritual for how to make your dreams come true, but if you don't bring in and really live under a Code of Life that is in alignment with the certain Universal forces and values, what you want will not come to pass. Similarly, you can live under a Code of Life that is honorable, compassionate, giving, loving, and of service to those near you, your community, or even the world and humanity as a whole, but without the proper tools, the true teachings you need, you will still not be able to create and manifest what you desire. It takes both, and this book gives you both: the practices for manifesting and the principles, the Code of Life, to ensure that the practices are not in vain and that all the effort and energy you put into creation actually materializes on this physical plane we call our lives. Both together are what have led me to bring all I want into my life. It will do the same for you.

Second, I want you to know that what I will share with you is not complicated. It will not take thousands of words to convey. The chapters that follow will be short, concise, and to the point. Hopefully, this will make what I write easy to get though, easy to digest, and easy to remember. But don't be fooled by their brevity. As we've all heard so many times: "Big things come in small packages." Take what I give you to heart and integrate it into you. Don't just read and say: "Wow, that's easy!" If it was that easy, everyone would have everything they want, and we know that's not the case. I encourage you to really make what I have to say part of your life, part of your DNA, part of *you*!

May you have all you desire.

Namaste

Part One

THE ART OF CREATION

1

Take the First Step—What Do You Really Want?

The most important question in life is this: What do I really want?

It sounds easy to answer. But it's not. In fact, it's one of the toughest questions in life to answer honestly.

And significantly, there is only one, yes *one*, answer.

You can't have a few answers. You can't say: "Well, in this part of my life I want this the most, and in that part of my life I want that the most."

This is one of the greatest errors people make in their efforts to manifest what they want in their life. It plays into one of the great principles of life, and manifestation. It goes like this.

Everything is made of energy. Energy, which is invisible, manifests into things, which are visible, material.

Thoughts are energy. That means, thoughts manifest into physical things. This one principle is how everything in your life is created. This is true whether you like what you've created or not. Your thoughts have created your life. I'll discuss this more in chapter 4, but you must pay attention to your thoughts, because what you think, you create, and if you're loose with your thoughts, you're loose with what you create and are likely creating things you don't really want.

☛ To create what you *do* want, you have to decide what that *truly* is. You have to decide on the *one thing* that you want *above all other things.*

The reason you need to choose one thing is that, again, thoughts are energy, and if you disperse the energy, if you send your manifesting energy into multiple areas, you dissipate that energy and its ability to manifest.

By analogy, let's say you have a valve that needs *X* pounds of pressure applied to open. You have one source of force, and that one source is enough to open the valve only if it is fully and exclusively applied to that one valve. But if you divide the force between two valves, there's not enough to open the one valve you really wanted to open because some of the force has been diverted to the other valve.

Thus, it is essential, critical to the manifesting process, that you answer the precise question: "What do I really want?" It is not a question asking for more than a single answer. It is not asking for an answer that says: "I want this, this, and this equally;" or "I want this a lot, and this too, and this, but a little less."

It's hard. I know. But you *must* choose, you *must* decide. You must pick the one thing you truly, really want to manifest. Without this, you are likely, if not doomed, to fail in your quest to create what you want.

Don't be afraid to admit that this is an extremely hard question to answer. Maybe not for all, but for most it is. For me, it was. It took me over a decade to answer this question. I had been wanting to get out of law for years. I took a shot at being a real estate broker; I had a broker's license and sat open houses. I applied to go back to school to become a family therapist. I started to paint, and even had a show at a prestigious gallery in Los Angeles where I sold my paintings. I set out to become a travel agent. It took me a loooooooong time to really come to terms with what I really wanted to do with my life. In fact, it took me giving myself cancer to force me to figure out the answer to this question.

Here, I must digress for a moment. Yes, you read that right, I did say, "I gave myself cancer." I fully believe this to be true. I created it. I caused the disease to manifest in my body. I did this because I couldn't figure out another way to leave the practice of law. I was always too scared, too tied to a lawyer's salary, too insecure to step into the abyss and let Life take care of me. So I stuck with the law, continuing to dream of leaving it one day. But I remember, distinctly, lying on the floor of my condo one afternoon, looking out the window and thinking: "If I don't get out of the law biz soon, I'm going to get sick." And sure enough, not long after, I got my cancer. I thought it, it happened. It's not rocket science.

This is how manifestation works, for both good and what appears to be not so good.

You can, and do manifest in this way as well. The trick, really the secret, however, is to take control of the manifestation process. And the first step to doing this is to answer the question: *What do I really want?*

Think long. Think hard. Meditate on this question if you meditate. Walk on the beach, walk in the mountains, go running. Do whatever you do. But think on this question as deeply as you possibly can to come up with the answer.

You may ask: "How will I know this is *the* answer? How do I know this is the *right* answer?" My response to you is this: Your answer will resonate with you. It will be like a harmonious note with your being, your soul, your inner self—whatever you want to call the core of yourself. You will know. It will just feel right.

In addition, it will be easy to visualize. I'll discuss this more in the next chapter, but what you really want will be easy to see in your mind's eye. It will be like hitting the right note and knowing it, if you sing. It will be like hitting the sweet spot in a golf shot, if you golf. It will be like finding the perfect piece of clothing or jewelry for that special occasion, if you shop (and we all shop!).

Lastly, I believe a good, if not the best, place to start in thinking about this question is to ask yourself: "What am I passionate about?" If you think deeply about this, I believe it will begin to move you toward securing the answer to the key question of: "What do I really want?"

Have fun with this. Don't rush it. But don't procrastinate with it. Think deeply. As was once said in a movie: "The answer is out there."

2

Practice Using Mental Imagery

You've decided what you really want. Now the question is: "What's next?" Here is the answer.

You need to visualize what you want, and follow the practice I will lay out. This will start the manifestation process.

First, you need to state what you want. You can use any group of words you choose. But in essence, you need to say, out loud, something to the effect of: "I will use all my energies to manifest the following desire: . . ." and then you need to fill in the end of the statement with "what you really want."

☛ Then, you need to visualize what you want. You should create as clear a picture as you can. Put it in as much detail as you can. Colors, smells, sounds all help.

I would suggest not trying to create the finished picture all at once. Leonardo da Vinci didn't paint the Mona Lisa all in one sitting. Start with a general outline of what you want. Over days and weeks, fill in details. Things will come to you as you fill in the picture.

Don't force it. And this leads to a critical point, which is this:

If what you decide you want to manifest, what you want to create, is not easily visualized, if what you think you really want doesn't form easily, fluidly, effortlessly in your mind, take some time to check back in with your desire, and make sure it is *really* what you want most, more than anything. Your goal should be easy to visualize. That's not to say every detail should be easy to visualize on the first day. But the general outline of it should. And as the days go by, it should be easy, in fact fun to fill in details of the picture. If it's not, if you feel like you're struggling to see what you desire, if you feel like you're swimming upstream against the current with this practice, then it is usually, not always, but usually a sign that you need to check back in with your desire to ensure it is, in the core of your being, "what you really want." Be honest with yourself. This is a must, and if you are certain that you know "what you really want," then continue to visualize it.

If it continues to take more than what you think is a reasonable amount of effort to visualize what you want, think about breaking your "want" into steps or stages. Make the desire bite size. For example, if you want a new job, and you can't visualize yourself sitting at the desk in your new job, then start by making your desire the preparation and mailing out of a resume. See if you can picture yourself finishing the resume, printing it, putting it into an envelope, putting the stamp on it, and dropping it into a mailbox. If you can visualize that, then make that your desire until you've sent out resumes. Then make the desire getting an interview. Picture yourself getting the call to set up an interview at a place you'd love to work. If you send out more than one resume, visualize a few different places from which the call could come. After you get the call, then make the desire having a great interview, and visualize that.

After the interview, make the desire getting the job, and visualize the call coming to you and getting the offer for the job.

You can do the practice this way, in segments, if it works better for you. For most, this approach is better, and easier. Either way, if your desire is aligned with where it is supposed to lie, the image will come.

Before getting to the final step in the practice, I want to add in one belief I have about imagery and the use of a mental image to manifest. Some, maybe many, will not agree with what I am about to say. And some may find it almost sacrilegious. That's okay. I just ask you to keep an open mind. And I ask you to continue to read on after you read what I am about to say: it is just my opinion, my interpretation of something, and it is not essential to the practice or to manifesting whatsoever. But I write it because I find it deeply significant for me, and potentially significant to others.

In the bible (Genesis 1:27) it is written: "God created man in His own image, in the image of God He created him; male and female, He created them." Most people read this to mean that, in some manner, man "looks like" God. That's why there are hundreds, really thousands of paintings and illustrations depicting God to look like a man, a human man. But I interpret this passage from the Bible differently. I interpret it as a key to manifestation. Because when I read it, I interpret the word "image" as a verb, not as a noun. I interpret it to say that God created Man using "its imagery," using "its imagination," using the same powers and process of visualization I am setting forth here. You create what you desire. In fact, as I said in the introduction, you create everything in your life with your mental images, whether you like it or not. You create in your image; the images in your mind. This is our God-given power. This is our birthright. This is a large, in fact *the* predominant factor in why we are human. I'll keep saying it: You create every minute of every day from the images you hold in your mind. These images create the physical reality around you. The key to manifesting, the key to having what you want in your life, is to take positive, intentional control of these images and create what you want.

This brings us to the last step in the practice. This is the step that intentionally puts in motion the wheels of manifestation.

Once you have the image of what you want in mind and you hold that image in your mind for a number of minutes (say, three to seven minutes, although there is no exact rule), take that image and mentally burn it into the back of your brain. It is like branding. Sear that image into the back of your head, inside the skull, and inside the brain, but in the back of the brain. Think of the inside, back of your skull as a movie screen, and project your image onto that screen. Do this twice a day. First very soon after you wake up and before you begin any of your daily routines, and second, just before you go to bed.

This practice will put the wheels of controlled, intentional manifestation into action.

3

Don't Doubt, Be Patient;
Faith Is the Key

Now, I must provide you with some cautions. Just because you do the visualization practice I've laid out, doesn't mean what you want will automatically manifest. There are pitfalls, traps you can fall into. I want you to avoid these traps, these hurdles to getting what you want. So, please pay attention to what I am about to write, because it is just as important as the practice itself.

☛ **Do not have doubts. Period.**

There are two aspects to this. Doubting the desire you set up is a sure recipe for failure. If you are not absolutely sure about "what you really want," then what you *think* you want is not going to happen. You have to be sure that what you say to yourself that you really want is, truly, "what you really want." If you doubt this, you're doomed from the outset.

It's even more difficult not to doubt the process. You have to have utter faith that the practice you are doing will work. If you don't, then you will inevitably stop the manifestation process. It is as simple as that: Doubt and you're done.

It has been said that worry is the worst form of meditation. (More about this in chapter 14.) But for now, just realize that when you worry, you focus. It's a worry, so you worry. You think about whatever you are worrying about over and over. Doubt can work the same way. You begin to doubt the process. You think, "It's not working." This thought then becomes your dominant thought, which kills the manifestation process as the dominant thought is always what manifests. It lingers in the back of your mind, like a ball and chain, like an albatross around your neck, hindering, slowing, if not collapsing the manifestation process. At best, doubt makes manifesting extremely difficult, and at worst, impossible.

So, be patient. While today's society is so much about instant gratification, the manifestation process is not. You need to have faith. That is the key. (More about this later in chapter 12.) You need to allow the process to unfold. We have allowed many images to unknowingly build up in our minds over many, many years. You are now taking steps to dissolve those images and replace them with ones you want, ones you have chosen. What took years to build up is not torn down in minutes, or days, or even weeks. Again, you need to be patient, both with yourself and the process.

I would add, don't say your goal over and over during the day. This is a sign of doubt. You're saying it because you're uncertain that you've done enough just by saying it twice a day. You think that more is better, that repeating the desire will help it become a reality. But the opposite is true. Say and visualize the goal twice a day, upon rising from bed and before going to sleep. That is all.

I would add one other thought to help you with doubt and faith. The first time you work on the practice of manifesting I've given to you will be the most difficult time you will have in holding back doubts and in holding forth faith. This is because you have nothing on which to base your faith in the process. Put simply, you are relying on the proverbial "blind faith." *But,* once you implement the practice and have it work, then the faith is blind no more. You've experienced the results. You've seen it work. You know you manifested what you wanted. This makes doing it again soooooooo much easier, and less full of doubt.

So again, the first time you use the practice to manifest what you want, be patient, and do your utmost best to hold back the doubts that will almost certainly creep in as you will not manifest what you want overnight.

Lastly, let me say this. Not everything you determine to be "what you really want," and then work to manifest using the practice, will, in fact, manifest. There can be any number of reasons for this. Your "imaged" desire may not be correctly aligned with your true, core desire.

Doubts may creep in. Life may bring you events that distract you from your desire. There is no guarantee. If you work at the practice, and continue to work at the practice, and do all you can to work at the practice for what you think is an extended period of time, and "it's just not happening," then stop and revisit the desire.

This may sound counterintuitive, or contrary to everything I've said about manifesting. But as I said in the introduction, every principle, every practice I've set out so far has worked for me; I am living proof these principles and practices work. They come from a long, long line of teaching, a deep well of wisdom. And they do work. In the end, however, you need to follow your own intuition and learn to know when an adjustment to your desire needs to be made. Work on knowing. Work on following your gut. When something just pops into your thoughts, acknowledge it, think about it, and decide whether it's something you should act upon. This will help you to develop your intuition, which, in turn, will help you to know "what you really want."

4

Watch Your Tongue, Watch Your Mind

I reiterate: you create every waking minute of every day—in fact, every second.

Even more specifically, with every word you utter, you create. This is because, whether you realize it or not, when you speak, you have a picture in your mind of what you are saying.

When you say, "I want hamburger for lunch," you actually have a picture of a hamburger somewhere in your mind. It may be subconscious, but it's there. When you say, "I have to go to the market to get groceries," you have a picture of the market somewhere in your mind. This happens automatically, every time you speak, even to yourself.

What is significant about this is that once again we are dealing with mental pictures, the visualization of images we want to create. Thus, when we speak, we are actually creating, because as we speak, we create images in our mind and those images create our reality.

This makes it critical to watch what we say, to watch our tongues. You can do all the visualization practices you want to manifest a car, but if you get out on the street and see the car you want and then say to the friend you are with: "Wow, there's the car I want, but I'll never get it, it's just impossible," you ain't gonna get the car. You've *kiboshed* the whole manifestation process by what you've just said.

This works for everything. If you want a new job, but repeatedly tell your co-worker, "I hate my job," all you are doing is creating a deeper and deeper job hole out of which to climb as your mental image in that moment is one of you hating your job, and that image is what will be, or continue to be.

This concept also applies to your thoughts when you are alone with yourself. Thinking internally, or talking to yourself, is the same as speaking out loud to someone else. Internal or external articulation of words is the same. The articulation is a thought, and a thought is energy, and energy creates. So, whatever you are saying, or thinking, is creating whatever you are thinking or saying. It's unavoidable.

☛ You need to watch your thoughts and your words. We usually don't. We usually think random things or just blurt out random words. This unguarded, unrestrained thought is usually the single-most common cause of a sabotaged manifestion process.

So be vigilant, and pay attention to what you are saying and thinking. Pay particular attention to your use of the word "can't." Can't is a killer. It stops all action. It's like a brick wall. Thus, and simply: take the word "can't" out of your vocabulary.

Instead, do your best, really your utmost, to think only positive thoughts, thoughts that work with, rather than against, what you want to manifest. Regular, repeated use of affirmations—statements to yourself and to the Universe that begin, "I am . . ." and end with what you want—are very helpful and can help to maintain a positive thought pattern. Conversely, do not intentionally think negative things, toward what you desire, or toward others. Be mindful; you can work to manifest negatively, but if you do so, particularly if others are involved, there will be negative ramifications to you. I didn't coin the phrase, but it can be true: Karma's a bitch. Instead, stay positive.

5

We Are Creating Machines

As I have said before, we create every minute, really every moment we are alive. That's what we do. That is what being human is. We are creating machines. Our minds, our brains, are designed to create. Their purpose is to create. The physical universe was, and continues to be, created through mental imagery. You may not think so, nor want to believe it, but it is so. When you think deeply about this, you come to realize that maybe you are creating things you don't want to create. When you say negative things, when you think harmful thoughts, when you contemplate or share doubts with others, you are creating these negative, harmful, doubting things. They do manifest.

Trust me. I know. I did it to myself. I gave myself cancer. I said these exact words to myself. I remember them so clearly, "If I don't get out of law, I am going to make myself sick." Within a year, I was sick. And keep in mind, I said some of the strongest manifesting words one can say, "I am." Spiritual teachings from so many traditions instruct us to say affirmations on a regular basis to help us manifest what is affirmed. Not surprisingly, they often guide us to begin the affirmation with "I am." I did this, (and importantly, I did this without paying attention to what I was actually doing), and it further accelerated the creation of my illness.

So be careful, be watchful, be consciously aware of, and really tuned into *all* that you are thinking, *all* that you are saying. Because with each thought, with each word, you are directing the Universal Energy to take action and start forming into physical existence what you think and say.

☛ This is why, in every moment, you must be consciously aware of, and pay attention to what you think, say, and do. Because what you think, say, and do becomes, or lays the foundation for it to become a reality in your life.

Part Two

A CODE
OF LIFE

6

The Universe Will Always Provide

The Universe, the Universal Energy, God, if you prefer, will always bring you what you need. It may not always be what you want, but it will be what you need.

If we are in alignment with our true purpose, where we are supposed to be heading in our life, then what is provided will seem like, "Ahh, this is just what I needed." When we are not in such alignment, then what is provided will seem more like, "Ugh, this isn't what I wanted to happen." But in fact, even if something doesn't seem like it was what we wanted, it is, in fact, what we needed. That is why it happened. We were out of alignment with our true purpose, and some seemingly negative event was needed to get us off the path we were on and onto a new path to get us going, once again, in the right direction.

☛ Put simply, the Universe will provide you with whatever you need, whether you like what you need or not. This is the principle that gives us our life challenges.

Sometimes, we need to experience something we don't find too pleasant in order for us to grow. It is basically a kick in the rear. Life is really all about growing, expanding, evolving. It is about climbing the ladder, about reaching that next level. In actuality, personal evolution is an upward spiral. You will find challenges in life, and as you pass one, another comes. It's a different challenge, and a bit more challenging than the last. You've moved up and around the spiral. Eventually you make it all the way around, and you have a challenge that's similar to a prior challenge, but definitely more challenging. You're up the spiral, but all the way around and right above where you were in the past.

These challenges will keep coming. This is what life is about. Even others whom we may think have it easy have their own challenges. Have you known an ultra-wealthy person? Is their life perfect? Are they without challenges? No. Getting money may not be their challenge, but they have other challenges, like how to control their spending or how to respond to requests from loved ones for "help." Do you know a highly successful professional? They may not have professional challenges, but they may have challenges in their personal relationships with their spouse or their children. We all have challenges. And we always will.

But this leads to a second great spiritual principle. You may have heard the saying: "Everything happens for a reason." Actually, everything happens for a *good* reason. So, as things come up, as things happen in your life, keep this in mind. Whatever is happening is happening to help you grow, to evolve, to take you to a higher level. The happening may not seem good in the moment it is occurring, but at some point, maybe way down the road, you will find there is a good, positive reason for it.

Next, the Universe will always bring you what you need to take you back to The Middle Pillar. You might call this The Middle Way or The Middle Path. But the essence of the idea is that when you stray too far off the place of balance in your life, (for it is in the middle that balance is achieved), the Universe, Life, will bring you back to that place. And again, this rebalancing will occur whether you like it or not.

And this leads to a key point that ties many things together. If you don't stray too far from the Middle, the events that occur to put you back on The Middle Path won't be so harsh. We will stray. Again, that's part of life. This is what leads to the challenges that grow us. But the events that will occur to get us back to the middle will be like a gentle nudge, instead of a smack upside the head.

Finally, and directly related to the practice of manifestation, it is important to understand how whatever you desire is actually provided: how it comes into existence; how it manifests is for the Universe to work out, not you. For example, if you want a new car or a specific vacation, but you think you don't have the money for it, don't let that stop you from setting that as your desire.

It is your job, as a human being working to manifest, *to set up the desire.* It is the job of the Universe to take the energy of the mental pattern of the desire you set and transform that energy into a reality on this physical plane. It is key that you *do not* think about, worry about, or concern yourself with "how is this going to happen?" It is the job of the Universe, the way Universal energies and laws work, to transform your desire into a physical reality. The Universe will provide whatever is needed to make your desire manifest if you work the practice correctly. That's just the way it works.

But there are a few caveats. First, what I would call crazy, long shot things like winning the lotto or having a specific horse or sports team prevail so you can win a bet simply won't happen. The manifestation practice won't work on outside events like this.

Similarly, you can't manifest someone loving you. You can't have a crush on someone, and then apply the manifestation practice in the hopes of turning the crush into a relationship. You can use it to create a relationship for yourself as that is about you. But you cannot make lotto balls come out of the tube, or make a quarterback throw an interception, or make someone love you.

☛ Finally, be open, be flexible, don't be rigid. What you ask for may come in a form that's not exactly what you asked for, not exactly what you expected. But its essence will be there. Be open to see it, and receive it.

For example, you desire a car. Maybe you want a new blue, four-door sedan. You visualize this. You see yourself driving it in, you smell the new car smell, and you hear the radio playing as you drive your blue four-door. Then suddenly, out of nowhere, a friend says they got a new job in Dubai, but they had just bought this red, two door SUV and they want to give it to you or sell it to you at a very reduced cost. It has a few miles on it, but it's like new. Do you turn your friend down saying it's not the exact blue four door sedan with zero miles you envisioned? I hope not. You should really look at what the essence of your desire is. Is it the color? Is it the number of doors or number of miles? Probably not. You've manifested the essence of your desire, but it's a little bit different than what you pictured. Accept that; unless there's really something off from what you wanted.

Similarly, if you want a four-bedroom house with a walk-in closet and a pool, but a five-bedroom home at an amazingly low price but with no walk-in closet or pool is presented to you. Don't reject it out of hand because a few things are not exactly what you wanted. Maybe you can build the walk-in closet or the pool with the money you saved because the price is so low. Again, don't be rigid. Manifestation is not an exact science.

I'll finish with a story I heard that I think will crystallize this idea for you.

There's a man who owns a home near a river, and there's a terrible storm. For days and days it rains. Finally, he realizes that he has to leave his home as the water is rising and rising. His home is a lost cause, and if he doesn't leave he will drown as the home is now surrounded by rising water. He cries out to God, "God,

I need a miracle, please save me from the rising water, I don't want to die." Soon, a person in a canoe comes by and says "Get in, I've come to rescue you." The man, now on the roof of his home, says back, "No, I'm waiting for a miracle from God to save me. You're just a guy in a canoe." So, the person in the canoe paddles on. Hours go by and the water continues to rise. Then a person in a motor boat sees the man on the roof and says "Hop in, I've come to rescue you." Again, the man on the roof says "No, I'm waiting for a miracle from God to save me, you're just a guy in a boat." And, the motor boat motors on. Finally, with the water so high that the man on the roof is at its peak, a helicopter comes by and drops a rope down with the person in the helicopter yelling down "Grab the rope, we've come to save you." Again, the man on the roof rejects the rope, shaking his hand, waving the helicopter off, thinking, "A helicopter is no miracle, I've been a religious man all my life and I'm going to wait for a true miracle."

But no "miracle" comes. The water rises. And the man drowns. He finds himself in heaven, facing God.

He says to God: "God, I've been a religious man all my life, I've prayed, gone to my place of worship, and have been a good husband, father, and friend. Why didn't you create a miracle to save me?" God responds: "Dude, I sent a canoe, a motor boat, and a helicopter. What more do you want? You don't see that was a miracle? Who gets three cracks at having their life saved? Most get none. A few get some. You got three. Who were you waiting for? God?"

And that's just it. Don't hold out for the exact thing you desired. It may be slightly different in size, shape, color, smell, feel, and so on. Look at the essence of what's presented to you. If the essence of what you wanted is presented, grab it. It won't stay there forever.

7

Watch for the Small, Everyday Miracles

What is a miracle? The sky opening and God talking? A chorus of angels singing to you? An instant healing you experience or watch? A guru levitating? A boat lost at sea being discovered by a search plane or a lost hiker finding a path back to town? Maybe it's slowing down or stopping your car for some unknown reason just before you get into an accident. Is it being at a desk right when the call comes to offer you a new job, because if you weren't there the offer would have gone to another? Or maybe it's unexpectedly stumbling across the perfect new home you were looking for when you weren't even really looking?

I have to digress here and relate a few stories of my own because I think the concept of miracles, and the fact that they really do happen all the time, but we just don't notice them or call them something else, is so, so important to creating a better life for one's self.

Many years ago, when my daughter was a young child, my then wife and I took her to see the play *Beauty and the Beast* as it was her favorite book and video. After the play was over, I called my best friend to tell him how great the play was and that he should take his children. At the end of the call he said, "Hey, you need to check out the house next to me, it just went on the market and it's amazing. You should buy it. We could be neighbors!" I responded, "I'm not looking to move; I like the house I'm in and there is no way I can raise the money to buy a new home." He said, "Just take a look, trust me, you'll love it." I thought, "Sure, why not, it's just a weekend afternoon, and I like looking at new houses."

I drove to the house and called the number on the real estate sign, and lo and behold, the broker said, "Great, I can be there in fifteen minutes." We waited, the broker arrived, and we went in. I was floored. It was one of the most magnificent homes I had ever seen. I said to my then wife, "We have to get this house!" She agreed.

While, as I said before, I didn't have any idea in that moment how I could make this happen, how I would get the money to buy this large, beautiful home, I put the manifestation practices I have written above into action, and within a matter of weeks I had moved and began creating some of the best memories of my life, living right next door to my best friend with our children growing up together. To me, particularly looking back on what transpired, it was a miracle. Who gets to live in a dream home next to their best friend? I did. I lived that miracle.

More directly related to Mystic Journey Bookstore, it was late summer of 2008, my bout with cancer was in the rear-view mirror, and I had decided to open the bookstore. To do this, I had to put together a pool of money to cover the build-out costs and secure our start-up inventory. Part of that pool was to come from an equity line of credit I had with IndyMac bank. Then, one day, before I had drawn out the money I needed to start the bookstore from the line of credit, I was driving my car listening to the radio, really channel surfing the stations to find something I liked. Out of the corner of my ear, I heard something about IndyMac bank. I turned my focus to the radio, and I began to hear a full report on how IndyMac bank was about to close, and close tomorrow! I immediately pulled over and gathered my thoughts. If IndyMac closed, I would not be able to open the bookstore, as without the money from my equity line of credit, I wouldn't have the funds to get everything started. In that moment, I decided I needed to go home, get an equity line of credit check, and go to the bank and deposit it. I did just that. I took every dollar I could out my equity line of credit that afternoon. The next day, IndyMac bank shut down.

This sequence of events was a miracle. I happened to be in the car—the only place I listen to the radio—when the report came on. And I happened to be listening to the station that carried the report at the right moment even though I had been channel surfing just before between half a dozen stations or more. And I heard the report, rather than having my mind focused on something else and missing it. Finally, I listened to my Inner Voice and acted, I did not hesitate. It was a huge step, involving six figures. Everything transpired in just a few hours. If everything had not lined up just perfectly in those few hours, Mystic Journey Bookstore would not have been created. This book would not have been written. My whole life would have been different. This whole thing, the whole sequence of events was a miracle.

Lastly, I want to relate a story that will hopefully start to expand what your definition of "miracle" will encompass. I had just started selling large crystals and geodes at the bookstore when a customer came in and wanted to buy the largest crystal I had. In fact, it was the highest priced item in the store and would be the largest sale we had ever had. At the time, I really needed the sale. I worked out a deal with the customer, but I had to figure out how to transport and place this very large crystal in the customer's home as I had never done this before and had no one else to do it. I asked the customer to please give me a week or so to see whether I could resolve this issue and they said "okay." Days went by and I could not find anyone to transport and place the crystal. I was about to call the customer and tell them I couldn't deliver the crystal to them, and if they did not have someone to do this, we would have to forego the sale. But then one afternoon, there was a knock on the back door of the bookstore. I wasn't expecting anyone, but I went to answer it. The person at the door said, "I am here to pick up the crystal and deliver it for you." I responded, "Are you sure you are looking for Mystic Journey Bookstore? I didn't call anyone to pick up and deliver a crystal." We talked some more and figured out the person who knocked was supposed to pick up a large geode from a business across the street and take it from that business to that business owner's home. The delivery person was thankful I helped him get to the right place, but I said to him, "Hey, I have this crystal over here, can you deliver to one of my customers later this week?" He said "Sure." And boom, my delivery problem was solved. To me, this was a miracle. Who has someone who can do a very specific, very unusual task show up at their back door to do just what they need? I did! It was a miracle, and we consummated the sale.

Miracles are in the mind of the observer. Miracles are "miracles" only because of the particular label we attach to some event. Usually these labels come from what we were taught or told while we grew up. Thus, what is a miracle to one person is not to another.

☛ But, if we expand our definition of "miracle" and allow smaller things to be seen as miracles, *really* miracles rather than coincidences, then, *and this is so important to creating the life you want,* "miracles" begin to happen all the time.

When we become aware that miracles can happen all the time, then we are more open to them. When we are more open to them, they begin to happen to us more often. As we realize they are happening to us, faith builds that miracles can and will happen, and happen often. We then begin to believe that there is something out there watching over us, something that is good, being our guide and protecting us. Then more good things, more miracles happen, and life seems to get better and better.

Finally, as you begin to see more large and small miracles happen more frequently, you also begin to truly see what you might call everyday events bring you a deep sense of joy. Express your gratitude to the Universe for them. When you see a beautiful sunset, or taste a delicious meal, or have a warm embrace with you partner, child, or even your friend, say "thank you Universe, I am grateful to you for bringing me this moment." Love the moment, inhale it, feel—really feel—the gratitude for having the experience. As with miracles, when you express gratitude for what might be called a simple joyous event, an event that is often overlooked or taken for granted, they will occur more and more often and bring more and more joyous events and joy into your life.

8

Everything Is One Universal Energy

Everything is One. When we drill down to the smallest, littlest, tiniest particle of physical existence, it has the same aspect that comprises everything. This may not be the proper scientific way to say it, but this energy is at the core, at the foundation of everything. Nothing is not it. It is everywhere. It is everything. It is the Universal Energy, what some call God. Of course, if you prefer to use a phrase like the Life Force or some other title you want to give the omnipresent animating vibration that exists, that is perfectly fine.

☛ People have all sorts of names for this Energy or God. The name doesn't matter. But whatever you call *It*, *It* is everywhere and *It* makes up everything. Thus, everything is the same, everything is One.

Even *you* are an aspect, a spark of this One, this Universal Energy, this God, here on this physical plane. For if everything is One, then you must a part of that One as well. This is as true for you as it was for all of the great spiritual or religious figures. All are the same, the same as you too, but different. The iconic figures, yes, were further along the path, the spiritual path, than me or you. But we are still all the same at our core, at the smallest, tiniest, sub-atomic level.

Ultimately, we need to see religion, or religious and spiritual teachings and paths, as simply different spokes on a single wheel all leading to the same center. Each spoke is different. No two are exactly the same. Some provide support in one way, others in different ways. But all provide support for the wheel as a whole. All lead to a single center.

Put in more tangible terms, some of the spokes are colored, others send out different tones. Not surprisingly, some people resonate with some tones, while others are attracted to different colors. This is no different from certain people being attracted to diverse religious or spiritual teachings. The spokes are separate, but they support each other. They don't harm each other. And they all connect to one single center. That one single center is the Universal Energy, God.

If this Universal Energy is everywhere, comprising everything and everyone on this physical plane, then it follows that everything must be good. For why would this Universal Energy want to do evil unto itself. Some things may appear not good: war, poverty, abuse. But after some period of time, even these apparently bad things will lead to something that unfolds that is good.

This leads into the age-old question: Why do we have to go through bad experiences to get to some good deeper meaning? What's the point of this up and down life? In fact, why are we here at all? The answer to these questions is this: we, humans, exist on this physical plane so that the Universal Energy can experience itself on this plane of existence. The Universal Energy is everywhere, everything, on *all* planes of existence. Experiences on each plane of existence are different. On this physical plane in which we live, the Universal

Energy experiences itself through its living creatures, including us humans. It hears through our ears, sees through our eyes, feels tactilely though our hands. We are this Universal Energy, we are God. So, in whatever we are doing, God experiences itself through us on this physical plane. And the Universal Energy wants to experience all of itself that it can, good and bad. Thus, we have life's challenges, its ups and downs. The Universal Energy experiences these things, with the ultimate desire to make its creations on the physical plane exist as close to the perfection of the Universal Energy, God as itself, such that the evolution of humankind trends toward, and will eventually meet and live in, this perfection.

9

Be Tolerant of Others and Their Beliefs

As all is One, shouldn't it follow that all aspects of that One support and nurture all other aspects of that same One? A famous song from the '60s was called, "What the World Needs Now is Love." In my view, what the world needs now is tolerance. We need to learn to accept all the spokes of the wheel that I just mentioned.

This applies not only to religious or spiritual beliefs, but also to lifestyles and values. It would so help our world if we would stop thinking that our way, our view, is the best way, or worse yet, the only way. Or that if someone doesn't follow what we say or think, they are wrong. The "my way or the highway" philosophy is dividing us.

I think we can all agree that if someone says "I like apples," and another says "I like oranges," the two won't end up in an argument or a fight, or even a disagreement about which is better, or that you can enjoy only one and not the other. It's a matter of taste, literally. Why not the same about religion or lifestyle.

If one person resonates with the teachings of Jesus, why shouldn't they be allowed to follow his teachings? Same with Buddha. Or Mohammed. Or Moses. Or Lao Tzu. Different teachings resonate differently with different people. The same is true in school. One student likes math. Another excels at English and writing. A third is a science wiz. We never say to children you can't study math or English or science. Why is religion or lifestyle different?

Of course, if someone's religion or lifestyle is harming you, or impinging on your freedom, then no, that should not be tolerated. But otherwise, it would be great if we could all just open up, relax, let everyone do their own thing. Why not? What harm is there in this?

In the same vein, what gives anyone the moral or other superiority to judge another? Who can say they know better? Who has ordained themselves the Grand Master of Knowledge and Right Thinking? It is far better to look at one's self and not judge others. How can anyone judge another individual when they have no way to know what the other person has been through or is thinking or what has brought them to the place they are in life at any given moment? Just accept and focus on the positives in the other person and on yourself. For in the end, you only have control of yourself, your actions, and your thoughts.

10

Take Full Responsibility for All Your Actions

☛ What you have created in your life is yours. You did it. You created it. No one else. You. You were in control.

You can't pawn off the responsibility for anything that has happened or is happening in your life to someone else or some external, outside event in life. You have to grasp it, own it, use it. All things that happen, happen for a reason, a good reason, and happen to grow you, to evolve you. See all things as such. Then they don't look as bad.

Shirking responsibility for what is happening and has happened in your life is a sure recipe for being stuck, or worse yet, repeating the series of events that led to what's unfolding before you. It will repeat, again and again, so that you have a chance to make a new choice, and take responsibility for that choice.

At some point in our lives, most of us have said to ourselves, "The same thing keeps happening to me." We get the same kind of job over and over. Our love relationships seem to have the same recurring themes. People with selfish agendas keep coming into our lives. This is occurring because we are not taking responsibility for events that led to the situation arising in the first place. We are not digging deep enough to understand the underlying cause of what is appearing in our lives. More importantly, we are not really searching for, not really listening to our intuition to hear, see, feel, and truly grasp the deeper meaning of what we are experiencing, what we are to learn from it, and how we are to grow from it.

☛ Why do some people escape poverty, overcome abuse, survive divorce or death, and thrive? It is grounded in taking responsibility for what has occurred, is occurring, and what they desire to occur going forward in their lives.

11

You Know Right from Wrong

As you take responsibility for everything in your life, past, present, and future, you also need to acknowledge and live from the understanding that you know right from wrong. You do. It's not a hard call. Most times, you don't need to even think about it. You know it, you feel it. You know what the right choice, the right action, the right path is. Here I am speaking primarily about the small, everyday, moment-to-moment decisions we make all the time. These are decisions that affect not only you but also others. They can involve your workplace, your family, your friends. The guiding light here is this: do not harm others mentally, emotionally, or physically. But this also applies to yourself.

You know when you are taking an action that will upset others, when there is a different path, a path that can lead to the result you want without causing harm or creating conflict with another. You know when you are doing this. You really do. Why are you taking this more adversarial route? Is it really necessary?

The same is true for actions dealing solely with yourself. You know, in fact you often say to yourself, "This isn't right, but . . ." or "This isn't the best choice, but . . ." or "I should do this, but . . ."

☞ Following the course of action you know to be right is a key step, a key building block in your house of manifestation.

Put conversely, when you take an action that you know is not right, that there is something wrong with your decision or action, you weaken your house for manifesting from the start. The bottom layer of bricks is unsturdy, uncertain, and unable to support what will be built on top of it.

This does beg the question, "What is right?" But this goes back to what I said previously: the compass, which is really a moral compass for making right decisions, starts with the concept that you should not make any decision or take action that will harm others, or yourself. It's pretty much the Golden Rule: "Do unto others as you would have them do unto you." For yourself, it's said "Do unto yourself as you would have others do unto you."

You know how you want to be treated. You know when someone has treated you wrongly. As I said at the beginning, it's not hard. Follow this principle and your house of manifestation will have the strongest possible foundation.

12

Integrity Is the Foundation of Manifestation

Integrity, your integrity, must be at the core of your being. Nothing is more important.

You might ask, "What do you mean by integrity?" The dictionary definition of integrity begins with, "The quality of being honest." What I am referring to is larger. It includes, "your word." The two are intertwined.

To "give your word" is to promise something to someone else. A "promise" is a declaration that you will do a particular thing. Significantly, this declaration is two-fold. First, it is a declaration to the person to whom it is being made. That person can even be yourself. Second, it is a declaration to the Universe.

Let me be blunt, because bluntness is called for here: If you can't keep your word, your house of manifestation is built on quicksand.

When you give your word, the person you give your word to is relying on it. They count on you to abide by what you said. If you don't follow through, they lose faith in you. They begin to not trust you. They don't believe you truly mean what you say.

The Universe is the same way. If you don't keep your word, then the Universe starts to not trust you, it doesn't believe that you want to, or will, follow through with what you say. What follows from this is that when you tell the Universe "what you truly want," the Universe is relying on you to be honest, to tell it "what you *truly* want." If you have been lying a lot, or even a little in your daily life, and the Universe has come to not trust that you mean what you say, then it will not respond, it will not create, it will not manifest what you say you want, because really, your actions have evidenced that you probably don't want it.

This principle is true, maybe even more true for the "small things," the mundane things in life. When you say to someone, "I will meet you at *X*," and you can't meet this most basic agreement, (and remember, this agreement is also with yourself, not just the other person), then how can you possibly meet your agreement that you have faith in and no doubts about what you profess you truly want to manifest.

If you and the Universe lose faith in your follow-through on your promise to others (or even yourself), to make those promises happen, how in the world can you and the Universe have faith in the materialization of what you want to manifest?

☞ **Nothing can be more key, more critical, more utterly foundational to manifesting than your faith in the certainty of the outcome you want to manifest.**

Yes, there are emergencies, and at times we cannot avoid missing a commitment we have made to others or ourselves. In these situations, slack must be given.

But in the vast majority of instances, our failure to meet a commitment we have given is by our own choice, whether that choice be to do something, or fail to do something that results in us being unable to keep the promise we made.

The question then becomes: was the commitment, the promise, you gave with your word a lie? Was it an untrue statement with an intent to deceive? This would be even worse than not following through with your word—even more out of line with one's integrity.

Just as we all know right from wrong, we also know, and maybe more readily know, when we lie. Telling lies erodes the bonds of energy that are needed to manifest. Again, you know when you are lying. And when you lie, you are not centered, you are completely out of balance. You don't trust yourself. And if you can't trust yourself, how can you trust yourself to not only practice the discipline necessary to manifest, but also to trust that you are manifesting what you really want, what is in line with your highest purpose?

☛ If you can't trust you, how can the Universe trust you?

When you lie, you look down on yourself, you doubt yourself. As I said above, doubt is one of the biggest roadblocks to manifesting. It doesn't matter the size of the lie. Even "little white lies" are just that, lies. They eat at the core of your being. They grind down the essence of your spirit. They sap your energy.

In the end, manifesting is about having inner honesty and integrity. It is about being true to yourself about what you really want, and then being honest in your commitment to do everything possibly necessary to make what you really want manifest on the physical plane. Acting with, thinking with, desiring with integrity, facilitates the manifestation process. It is greased. It is eased. Lying, the antonym to being honest, erodes, and in the end, stops all manifestation that is in alignment with one's true purpose.

13

Don't Give Negative Energy
to Anything

Even when you are certain that you have acted with integrity, taken the right path, and made the right decisions, seemingly bad or negative things may still happen to you. They are supposed to. They take place to help you grow. But don't give them any energy. This is key. Let them pass over you. Let them pass through you. Focus on the positive they can bring.

If you have an ache in your body, don't focus on it. Don't keep touching that part of the body. If you have a poor relationship with a co-worker, don't keep taking actions to get back at them, or on the other side, over and over, trying to fix it. If you have a friend that doesn't really seem to be a friend, someone who is not doing or giving or supporting you in a way that you know a friend should, don't give that friendship any more energy.

Instead, keep the mantra "All happens for a *good* reason" in the forefront of your mind. Remember, there is always some good reason, some good purpose for all that happens. It may not be easy to see at first, but it will appear eventually.

☛ There are no accidents, no mere coincidences. Everything that happens is there to grow us, to evolve us, to push us to the next level. If you are in alignment with your true purpose, synchronicities will appear.

Please recall my story about hearing the IndyMac announcement on my radio. It was no accident that I happened to be at the exact right place at the exact right time (in my car, listening to the radio, to the right station, at the moment of the announcement) to hear what I needed to hear. I was in alignment with my purpose, the creation of Mystic Journey Bookstore. The Universe knew this was what I was intended to be doing and provided me with what I needed in that moment. It was no happenstance accident. It was a divine synchronicity. Once you are aware of these synchronicities occurring, they will happen, or appear to you more frequently. And as they happen more frequently, they will aid in your growth, your evolution, your walk down your path.

14

Worry Is the Worst Form
of Meditation

Another form of negative energy is worry. There is nothing more negative, more opposed to manifesting what you want than worrying. Worrying is a focus on something negative or potentially negative. It is really a meditation on the negative because when most people worry they stop their mind, clear it, and let nothing else in but the worry. Then they dig deep into the worry, hoping for some answer to it, as people often seek answers in meditation.

The key thing here is that in meditation you are reaching into a plane of existence that is different, apart from our normal plane of physical existence. And that plane you are reaching into is the creative plane. It is the plane from which manifested reality on the physical plane emanated.

☛ When you worry, you reach into this creative plane with a negative thought, focused on that worry, and thereby your work is manifesting the negative thought, instead of your positive desires.

Be sure not to fall into this trap. Keep your thoughts, what you have put out into the Universe, conscious, consciously positive, and in alignment with what you truly want.

15

It Is Impossible to "Try"

To "try" is impossible.

☛ You don't try. In fact, you can't try. Either you do, or you don't. And thinking you are trying is another block to manifestation.

This is because manifesting involves doing, it involves doing the needed practices, not trying them. You don't try to find a job. Either you are looking for a job or not. You are not trying to look. You are doing it. In basketball, you are not trying to make a basket, you are shooting, and either making a basket or not. You don't try to come up with an idea for a new app or a new product. You are either coming up with it or not. You are not trying to come up with a new way to increase sales. You are either taking action to create new sales, or you're not. Think about it. You're not trying to walk. Either you're walking or you're not. You are either doing, or you're not. Period. There is no half way. Just take the word "try" out of your vocabulary and how you perceive your actions.

16

Don't Put Things Off

When something needs to be addressed, address it in that moment. Don't put it off. If it can't be handled in the moment, do it as soon as possible. Putting things off is a statement to yourself that you are avoiding something. It is a message that you don't want to take responsibility for acting on something that needs to be handled. Most importantly, it is a sign to the Universe that you don't care about it.

As you put more and more things off, they tend to build up. As they build up, they get even less likely to be handled, and if they are handled, then they are not handled in the best fashion. As things build up, so does pressure to deal with them, and so does the guilt for, and the worry about, not dealing with them. This not only leads to poor judgment in handling the issue when you finally deal with it, but also the worry takes your focus and energy from what you truly want to manifest and diverts it to the unwanted worry of what you really don't want and don't want to face.

☞ If something needs to be dealt with, deal with it. Taking care of the issue will make you feel better about it and yourself, once it is done and off your plate.

This sends a signal to the Universe that you can handle things, and will handle things, and take responsibility for handling things. This leads the Universe to bring you more, and the more will bring you more of what you want.

17

Life Isn't Short,
But It Goes by Fast

People say life is short. Don't believe that. Not for an instant. This ties back to the idea that we can make choices in every instant. You can change your life in a moment. Every moment. Life isn't short. There are innumerable experiences we can have. And in fact, we do have them. We just don't see it that way.

What can be said, however, is that life goes by fast. The minutes, the hours, the days, the months, the years, they roll by. They seem to go by faster and faster. And they mathematically do. In the second year of your life, the second year is 50 percent of your life. A large part of your life. In the tenth year of your life, the tenth year is 10 percent of your life. Still a lot, but less. In the fiftieth year of your life, the fiftieth year is 2 percent of your life. Much less. And each following year is a smaller percentage of your overall life.

☞ So . . . *live life!*

It keeps going by faster and faster. And you can't get any moment back. As it is said, all there is, is the present. So . . . Live it. Grasp it. Love it. Experience it. That's why we're here. To experience.

18

The Only Thing Certain Is Change

We often hear the saying that, "The only things that are inevitable are death and taxes." In my view, the only thing that is truly certain is change. That's it.

You can choose not to pay taxes. There are consequences, but you can choose not to. And sometimes circumstances arise where you actually pay no taxes and get a refund! Some believe that there are beings, gurus, that never die. Instead, they consciously drop one body and move into another. Their soul, spirit, lives on; there is no "death."

☛ But change, this is different. It cannot be stopped. It happens in every single moment.

Atoms are constantly in motion. Even in apparently solid things, the atoms that comprise the solid thing are in motion. Slower, yes, but in motion. If motion truly ceased, our physical universe would come to an end.

Instead, the position of the atoms is always changing. Motion is always occurring, and with motion, change. Thus, in every instant, your life is changing. The question really is, are you in tune with the change? Are you in alignment, in the flow with the change? And are you the captain of the ship of change, in control of the change, or just a ship adrift, being battered about by the ocean of change?

Always remember, a ship without a rudder can never reach its destination. Winds of change will always be there, but with knowing what you truly want and using the practices I've laid out, you can steer through and actually use those winds to land on the shore of your manifested desire.

19

Don't End with "I Wish I Had . . ."

I simply refuse to be in my last moments of life saying to myself "I wish I had . . ." I can't think of much worse.

Life is here to live. Life is here to experience. Remember, we are the Universal Energy here to experience itself on this physical plane. If our purpose is to experience, then we should experience *all* we can while we are here. To be at the end of your life, at the end of an incarnation, and wish you had experienced more or different things, is to say you missed out on something.

 Anything is possible. Everything is possible. You can change your life to experience anything you want. It's just a choice.

We make choices that appear to constrain other choices. But that's just a perception. Those other choices remain available. We simply choose not to avail ourselves of those other choices—for whatever reason. But we can. The key is to make a choice that opens the doors for other choices we want to make, not a choice that closes the other doors we want to choose.

Truly, in the blink of an eye, you've lived many, many years and life is nearing an end. You look back. High school and college seem to have happened so quickly. You can't believe you've been in a job for X number of years. How did the children already finish college?!

Life goes by fast. Period. Let's round off and just say that an average life span is seventy-five years. In relation to the life of a country, the world, the universe, it's a drop in the bucket. It zips by, and is done. Before you know it, you're in a place where you can't do the things you once did, or you really can't do much at all and you are contemplating the end of life.

I wrote this book because I not only want to share what I know about how to manifest, but also to impart, in the strongest way possible, my philosophy that one never wants to near the end of life and say to themselves "I wish . . ." You can fill in the end of the sentence with whatever you like. But to me, and *the* reason I share my knowledge about manifesting, is that I, and hopefully you, never want to be thinking as you are about to pass on, "Geez, I wish I had done this or that."

Life goes by fast. There's really no time to wait to create what you want in your life. Whether it be a relationship, a new home, or a vacation to your dream locale, you don't need to, and shouldn't, wait to make it a reality. You can have it "now," with "now" meaning sometime in the reasonably foreseeable future. And remember, life can, and often does, change in an instant. It can be because of a tragic event, like a car accident. It can be unexpected, like being told you have a disease. But it can also be by choice. You can leave one job for another. You can exit a bad relationship. Or, you can choose to determine "what you really want" and begin the steps to start manifesting it. The process truly begins in an instant, an instant of choice.

We create every moment of our lives. Why not create what you really want? Why not create that beautiful relationship, that dream home, that perfect vacation? Why wait?

You may, and many do, have some excuse in your answer to these questions. I don't have enough money. I don't have enough time. I don't have the smarts or the looks or the personality. But these are truly just excuses.

You can have whatever you desire. Use the practices above, have no doubts, and the Universe will provide whatever you need—it's a spiritual fact, one of the deepest spiritual principles that exists.

20

Take Risks, Don't Be Afraid, It's Up to You

You now have the tools, the practices, to create what you want. You also have some principles to live by that will assist you in manifesting. And you know that life goes by fast.

☛ So . . . don't wait. Act. Take risks. Don't be afraid.

Fear of acting will always, and inevitably, result in some event occurring which will then force you to act.

Why let the Universe force you to act? Why be reactive? Why not take the reins, take charge, take action, and be the leader in your life? It's your life, why not be its director? Why just be the actor taking directions from outside? You can choose to be in the driver's seat. It's up to you.

When you do start choosing, be bold, be brave. It's part of the no "I wishes" at the end of your life.

The old saying: "Nothing ventured, nothing gained" is so true.

In fact, the greatest rewards, the greatest growth, comes from life's greatest challenges, from taking the biggest risks.

There is no need to take foolish risks. When you develop, and listen to your intuition, your Inner Voice, you will know what risks are foolish. If you have any doubts about it, your intuition will tell you.

There is no way to know what is going to happen to you today. You could walk out the door and get into your car in what will be the last drive you ever take. You could go to work and be informed layoffs are coming and you are part of them. You could go to the doctor for a routine physical and be told they have found a tumor. You never know what any day will bring.

But what you do know is that you can, with your own actions, change your life, instantaneously, for the positive. You can take that first step. You can do it by taking some action you have always wanted to take, or you can start the manifestation process by deciding what you really want, and then putting the visualization practice to work. It is there for you. It is up to you. Everything you ever wanted is there for you. But it takes effort, dedication, and most of all, emotion ladened desire. Be bold. Be determined. Be certain. You can and will make it happen. You can and will create what you desire.

☞ Take that first step. Begin the practice. Live your dreams.

Epilogue—What Is Happiness?

As people near the end of a life, I believe they are often asking themselves: "Did I get all I could out of this life? Was it fulfilling?" "Would I live this life the same way again?" But isn't the answer to all these questions really the answer to a different question: "Did I enjoy the days I lived? Was I happy?" Of all the questions we ask ourselves during the course of our lives, isn't the one most frequently asked: "Am I happy?"

The truth is that we are all looking to be happy, day-to-day, most of the time. But isn't this about the hardest thing to do? We are all searching for that elusive "happiness." We all want to be "happy." But do we even know what these words mean? Is there even a standard definition for them? Is it different for everyone?

Isn't it amazing that even the American Declaration of Independence speaks to the pursuit of happiness? The Declaration reads:

We hold these truths to be self-evident, that all men (and women) are created equal, that they are endowed by their Creator with certain unalienable Rights, that among these are Life, Liberty and the pursuit of Happiness.

What is the "pursuit of Happiness?" Why are we pursuing it? Why is it in the American Declaration of Independence? Why is it on a par with Life and Liberty?

Why have so many books been written about it?

We all know or have come to learn that simply getting what we want, particularly material things, doesn't necessarily bring us happiness.

Doesn't the question really go deeper then? What is it that will truly make us happy? Or fulfilled? And how do we get to that place moment-to-moment?

☛ The key is to realize that happiness *should not be the end goal*. Rather, happiness *should be the path* on which we travel to reach that goal.

For if happiness is the goal, two problems arise.

First, if happiness is the goal, what happens after you reach the goal. Most of us set goals in material terms. When we reach the goal, we move on to set another goal. If happiness is the goal and we reach it, do we simply move on from, and leave behind, happiness to pursue other goals?

Second, and maybe more importantly, if happiness is the goal, this means that you won't be happy until you reach that goal. That is not good.

Instead, *happiness must be the path on which you travel* to the goal. You walk the path every day. You are traveling down the path in every moment. Isn't it best to be happy on the way to reaching the goal? Doesn't that even make reaching the goal, if not less important, less impactful? Doesn't that give you less attachment to the goal and its outcome (a key spiritual principle), if you're happy all the time as you work toward the goal?

And if happiness is the path to the goal, then can't you focus more on what the goal is? Focus more on what you really want?

Doesn't releasing happiness as a goal free you up to look deeper into what would be truly fulfilling to you, and even into more deeply understanding the purpose of life? Wouldn't doing so allow you to open your mind more to being at the end of life and saying, "I lived a full life. If I had a chance to do it again, I would. I had a happy life."

But this brings us back again to, "What is happy?" What makes you happy? Think about that. Write it down. What are the key elements to your happiness? And remember, your happiness doesn't belong to anyone else. No one can tell you what your happy place is. And, no one has the right to judge what makes you happy.

Keep remembering, happiness is not the goal. It is the path to the goal. It is how you want to live, what you want to be feeling, what you want to be experiencing moment-to-moment.

Think back on your life. Think hard. What moments made you the happiest? What moments can you remember as being happy? If you can remember some moment, some event, some feeling that you associate with them that you call happy, particularly if it is long ago, that is something that is in touch with *your* core happiness.

How do you get it again? How do you strike the same key on the keyboard? And not just once, but over and over?

Hopefully there are multiple such events you can remember. Then you can strike different keys at different times. Maybe you can even strike multiple keys at the same time and play a chord. Eventually, if you can continue to strike the keys, you can play an ongoing symphony. You can have a life that you love to play, love to live, each day, each moment.

Why is happiness so seemingly fleeting? Why does it seem so hard to come by? And maintain?

Life is supposed to bring challenges. They are what grow us. But don't the challenges impact, if not eliminate happiness? How do we not only face but also live through the challenges and still be happy and retain our happiness? And this is true not only for life challenges but also for seemingly small, momentary challenges. How do we remain stable, centered, in a place of happiness when we're stuck in traffic and late to something? When a meeting doesn't go the way we want? When we get rejected? When we have an argument with someone? When we're a little, or a lot, short of cash? When the car breaks down? When illness occurs? When it rains on the day you planned to be outside in the sun? How do you maintain your happiness through these events?

This is the key. The key to happiness. Happiness is an emotion. It's a state of being. It is something that is created internally, and only internally. The truth is, happiness is just a label you put on how you feel in relation to how you react to something.

And you choose how to react. You choose the label you put on that reaction. Take responsibility for that reaction, and that label. It's yours. Own it.

Happiness is all about how you react to things. And how you react is completely, and solely within your control. I didn't say it would be easy to control, but your reaction to anything, and, thus, your happiness, is yours to control.

☛ You can do this.

About the Author

Jeffrey Segal, author, life coach, artist, and founder of Mystic Journey Bookstore and Mystic Journey Crystals, was raised and educated in Los Angeles. He went to Occidental College and then to law school at American University in Washington, D.C. After securing his JD in 1985, Jeffrey returned to Los Angeles and began what turned out to be a twenty-five-plus-year legal career.

Before beginning that career, however, Jeffrey failed the bar exam. This failure turned out to be one of the most profoundly positive events in Jeffrey's life. It was this failure that inspired Jeffrey to turn to a set of spiritual teachings he had been given, but had never looked at, to help him overcome the bar exam hurdle. These teachings, and the manifestation techniques contained therein, not only helped Jeffrey pass the bar exam the

next time, but they also became the guiding life principles he has used ever since to create all that he wanted
in his life. These teachings are the core of this book.

Jeffrey then began his legal practice. But after ten
years he started to become disenchanted. As time
passed, this feeling became disillusionment, lack of
fulfillment, and ultimately an intense desire to get out
of law. But the "golden handcuffs" were too tight. He
couldn't leave. That was until, after some twenty years
of practice, Jeffrey "created" a cancer in his body, a cancer to finally force him out.

While the doctors initially thought they had caught
the cancer early, a follow-up test revealed a lymph node
abnormality. The doctors wanted Jeffrey to undergo
chemotherapy. Jeffrey instinctively knew, however, that
this was not the right path for him. Instead, he chose a
course of natural/alternative healing. He put together
a team of healers, including an acupuncturist, a body-
worker, an energy worker, a traditional therapist, and
his ever-supportive then girlfriend to guide him to
guide him on his path of healing. After six months of

working with his team, the abnormality had completely disappeared.

It was during this time of healing that Jeffrey decided to leave the practice of law and follow his passion in the realm of spirituality and create Mystic Journey Bookstore. After the bookstore expanded to become the largest spiritual book and gift store in all of Southern California, Jeffrey opened Mystic Journey Crystals in 2017. Jeffrey now travels the world, going to mines and workshops in places as far away as Uruguay and Madagascar, to personally source the crystals and geodes that grace the Mystic Journey Crystal Gallery.

Jeffrey now says, with much pride, "I love what I do."

Connect with Segal online at *mysticjourneyla.com* or on Instagram: @mysticjourneyjeff.

Hampton Roads Publishing Company

. . . for the evolving human spirit

Hampton Roads Publishing Company publishes books on a variety of subjects, including spirituality, health, and other related topics.

For a copy of our latest trade catalog, call (978) 465-0504 or visit our distributor's website at *www.redwheelweiser.com* where you can also sign up for our newsletter and special offers.